Table of CONTENTS

Mexican Shrimp

MAKES: 6 servings | **PREP:** 10 minutes | **START TO FINISH:** 20 minutes

- **1 pound frozen cooked shrimp, thawed**
- **1 cup diced mango**
- **⅔ cup diced red onion**
- **½ cup ORTEGA Salsa, any variety**
- **¼ cup chopped fresh cilantro**
- **2 tablespoons ORTEGA Fire-Roasted Diced Green Chiles**
- **¼ teaspoon salt**
- **¼ teaspoon black pepper**
- **1 package (12-count) ORTEGA Taco Shells, any variety, broken into large pieces**

CUT tails from shrimp, if necessary. Slice lengthwise in half. Place in medium bowl.

ADD mango, onion, salsa, cilantro, chiles, salt and pepper; stir well to combine. Refrigerate at least 30 minutes or up to 2 hours. Serve with taco shells.

TIP

For a special presentation, serve the shrimp in stemmed martini glasses. Stand taco pieces upright in the glass for a pleasing garnish, if desired. For an even healthier option, use ORTEGA Whole Grain Corn Taco Shells.

Mexican Meatballs

MAKES: about 30 meatballs | **PREP:** 15 minutes | **START TO FINISH:** 30 minutes

- **3 ORTEGA Yellow Corn Taco Shells**
- **1 pound lean ground beef**
- **1 egg**
- **2 teaspoons ORTEGA Fire-Roasted Diced Green Chiles**
- **1 teaspoon ORTEGA Reduced Sodium Chili Seasoning Mix**
- **1 bottle (8 ounces) ORTEGA Taco Sauce, any variety**
- **¼ cup (1 ounce) shredded Cheddar cheese**
- **Chopped fresh cilantro (optional)**

BREAK taco shells into food processor and pulse several times to create about ½ cup taco shell crumbs. Place in large mixing bowl; add ground beef, egg, chiles and seasoning mix. Mix thoroughly. Form into 30 (1-inch) meatballs.

HEAT skillet over medium heat. Add meatballs; cook until they begin to brown. Carefully turn meatballs over and continue browning. Add taco sauce. Coat meatballs with sauce and simmer over low heat, uncovered, 10 minutes.

SPRINKLE meatballs with cheese and garnish with cilantro, if desired. Serve with toothpicks.

TIP

For variety, replace the ground beef with either ground chicken or ground turkey. For an even healthier option, use ORTEGA Whole Grain Corn Taco Shells.

Spicy Watermelon Salad

MAKES: 4 to 6 servings | **PREP:** 10 minutes | **START TO FINISH:** 10 minutes

4 cups watermelon, cut into ½-inch pieces

1 cup cantaloupe, cut into ½-inch pieces

1 cup blueberries

3 tablespoons minced fresh mint leaves

2 tablespoons ORTEGA Taco Seasoning Mix or 40% Less Sodium Taco Seasoning Mix

COMBINE watermelon, cantaloupe, blueberries, mint and seasoning mix in large bowl; toss well. Chill before serving.

TIP

For an attractive presentation for any occasion, serve the salad in a watermelon bowl. Cut the watermelon in half and hollow out the inside. If desired, cut small, diagonal triangles along the top of the watermelon bowl using a paring knife. Fill with the Spicy Watermelon Salad and chill before serving.

Chilled Avocado Soup

MAKES: 4 to 6 servings | **PREP:** 15 minutes | **START TO FINISH:** 15 minutes

- 4 ripe avocados
- 1 cup chicken broth
- ¾ cup sour cream
- 3 green onions, chopped
- 2 tablespoons ORTEGA Taco Sauce, hot
- 1 jar (8 ounces) ORTEGA Green Taco Sauce
- 2 cups water
- Juice of 1 lime
- ½ teaspoon salt
- Additional ORTEGA Green Taco Sauce (optional)
- ORTEGA Tostada Shells, broken in half (optional)

TIP

To remove pits from avocados without leaving behind a lot of the meat, cut the avocados in half lengthwise, and twist to separate the halves. Carefully stab the center of the pit with the edge of a paring knife blade, then twist slightly; the pit should come out easily.

CUT avocados in half and remove pits. Scrape avocado flesh into food processor or blender.

ADD broth, sour cream, green onions and 2 tablespoons taco sauce. Process using on/off pulsing action until ingredients are finely chopped.

ADD 1 jar taco sauce, water,* lime juice and salt. Pulse until evenly mixed, stopping occasionally to scrape sides of bowl with rubber spatula. Process 2 minutes or until smooth. Refrigerate at least 2 hours or until chilled before serving.

GARNISH with 1 tablespoon additional taco sauce and serve with tostada shells, if desired.

**Pour some of the water into the emptied jar and shake to release any trapped sauce; add to food processor.*

Chile'd Wedge Salad

MAKES: 4 to 6 servings | **PREP:** 20 minutes | **START TO FINISH:** 20 minutes

- **1 tablespoon vegetable oil**
- **1 cup chopped onion**
- **1 teaspoon Polaner® Chopped Garlic**
- **1 pound lean ground beef**
- **¾ cup water**
- **1 can (4 ounces) ORTEGA Fire-Roasted Diced Green Chiles**
- **1 packet (1.25 ounces) ORTEGA Taco Seasoning Mix**
- **4 to 6 ORTEGA Yellow Corn Taco Shells, crumbled**
- **1 head iceberg lettuce**
- **1 cup (4 ounces) shredded Cheddar cheese**
- **1 cup blue cheese dressing**

TIP

For a spicier dressing, substitute ORTEGA Salsa for some of the blue cheese dressing; mix with the dressing before serving.

HEAT oil in medium skillet over medium heat until hot. Add onion and garlic; cook and stir 3 minutes. Add ground beef; cook and stir 5 minutes or until beef is browned. Drain and discard fat.

ADD water, chiles and seasoning mix;* cook and stir 5 minutes or until thickened.

LINE serving plates evenly with taco shells. Cut core from lettuce; cut into wedges and place wedges on taco shells. Top evenly with beef mixture and cheese. Serve immediately with dressing.

**If desired, substitute ORTEGA 40% Less Sodium Taco Seasoning Mix.*

Rotisserie Chicken Burritos

MAKES: 10 burritos | **PREP:** 10 minutes | **START TO FINISH:** 20 minutes

- 2 cups shredded cooked chicken
- 2 cups cooked rice
- 1 cup ORTEGA Salsa, any variety
- 1 cup ORTEGA Black Beans, rinsed, drained
- 1 package (10-count) ORTEGA Flour Soft Tortillas or Whole Wheat Tortillas
- 1 cup ORTEGA Refried Beans
- 1 cup (4 ounces) finely shredded Cheddar cheese
- Fresh lime wedges (optional)

COMBINE chicken, rice, salsa and black beans in large skillet. Cook and stir over medium heat until warmed through.

WRAP tortillas with clean, lightly moistened cloth or paper towels. Microwave on HIGH 1 minute, or until hot and pliable.

DIVIDE refried beans evenly among tortillas; spread evenly in middle of tortillas. Top with chicken mixture; sprinkle with cheese. Fold ends of tortilla to middle, then roll tightly around mixture. Place on platter, seam side down. Repeat with remaining tortillas. Serve warm with lime wedges, if desired.

Double Cheeseburger Tortillas

MAKES: 4 servings | **PREP:** 10 minutes | **START TO FINISH:** 20 minutes

- 1 tablespoon vegetable oil
- 1 onion, diced
- 1 pound lean ground beef
- ½ teaspoon salt
- ½ teaspoon black pepper
- 1 cup ORTEGA Salsa, any variety
- 1½ cups prepared queso sauce or cheese sauce, divided
- 6 (8-inch) ORTEGA Flour Soft Tortillas or Whole Wheat Tortillas, warmed
- 3 to 4 tomatoes, sliced
- 1 cup shredded lettuce

TIP

For a great garnish, top the stacked tortillas with a pickle and olive spiked with a toothpick to resemble a real cheeseburger.

HEAT oil in medium skillet over medium heat. Add onion; cook and stir 4 minutes or until translucent. Add beef, salt and pepper; cook and stir, breaking up meat, until browned. Stir in salsa and ½ cup queso sauce until well mixed. Reduce heat to low; cook 5 minutes longer.

PLACE warmed tortilla on plate. Spread with 2 to 3 tablespoons queso sauce. Top with one-fourth of meat mixture. Arrange several slices of tomato on top and sprinkle with ¼ cup shredded lettuce. Add another tortilla and layer with 2 to 3 tablespoons queso sauce, one-fourth of meat mixture, tomato and ¼ cup lettuce. Top with third tortilla. Repeat steps for second cheeseburger tortilla. Cut layered tortillas in half to serve.

Salsa-Rice Stuffed Roasted Peppers

MAKES: 4 servings | **PREP:** 15 minutes | **START TO FINISH:** 35 minutes

- 4 green or red bell peppers
- 1 tablespoon olive oil
- 1 teaspoon Polaner® Chopped Garlic
- 2 tablespoons chopped fresh parsley
- 2 cups cooked rice
- 1 cup ORTEGA Salsa, any variety
- ½ cup (1 stick) butter
- 1 anchovy, minced

PREHEAT oven to 350°F. Coat 9-inch square baking pan with nonstick cooking spray.

ROAST bell peppers lightly; place on rack in broiler pan 3 to 5 inches from heat or hold over open gas flame on long-handled metal fork. Turn peppers often until blistered and charred on all sides. Transfer to plastic bag; seal bag and let stand 15 to 20 minutes to loosen skins. Remove loosened skins with paring knife. Cut off tops and scrape out seeds; discard.

HEAT oil in skillet over medium heat. Add garlic and parsley; cook and stir until garlic is fragrant. Stir mixture into rice in medium bowl. Add salsa; mix well. Divide rice mixture among bell peppers. Place in prepared baking dish.

MELT butter in saucepan over medium-low heat; cook and stir until butter is light golden brown. Remove from heat; stir in anchovy. Spoon evenly over bell peppers. Bake 10 to 12 minutes.

Taco Sliders

MAKES: 8 tacos | **PREP:** 5 minutes | **START TO FINISH:** 30 minutes

- 1 pound lean ground beef
- 1 can (4 ounces) ORTEGA Fire-Roasted Diced Green Chiles
- 1 packet (1.25 ounces) ORTEGA 40% Less Sodium Taco Seasoning Mix
- 4 slices American cheese, cut into quarters
- 8 ORTEGA Taco Shells, any variety
- 1 cup shredded iceberg lettuce
- 1 tomato, sliced
- 16 dill pickle chips
- ¼ cup mustard
- ¼ cup ORTEGA Taco Sauce, hot

TIP

For a delicious alternative, try making these with warmed ORTEGA Flour Soft Tortillas, and wrap up the filling before serving.

COMBINE ground beef, chiles and seasoning mix in medium bowl; mix well. Form into 16 small patties.

HEAT medium skillet over medium heat. Add patties; cook 4 minutes on each side or until done. Top each patty with cheese; cook 2 minutes or until cheese is melted.

FILL taco shells evenly with lettuce, tomato, 2 cooked patties and 2 pickle chips. Combine mustard and taco sauce; serve with tacos.

Baja Fish Tacos

MAKES: 10 tacos | **PREP:** 10 minutes | **START TO FINISH:** 20 minutes

- ½ cup sour cream
- ½ cup mayonnaise
- ¼ cup chopped fresh cilantro
- 1 packet (1.25 ounces) ORTEGA Taco Seasoning Mix, divided
- 1 pound (about 4) cod or other white fish fillets, cut into pieces
- 2 tablespoons vegetable oil
- 2 tablespoons lemon juice
- 1 package (10-count) ORTEGA Flour Soft Tortillas, warmed

SUGGESTED TOPPINGS

Shredded cabbage, B&G® Sliced Ripe Olives, lime juice, ORTEGA Taco Sauce, any variety, chopped tomato

COMBINE sour cream, mayonnaise, cilantro and 2 tablespoons seasoning mix in small bowl.

COMBINE fish, oil, lemon juice and remaining taco seasoning mix in medium bowl; mix to coat fish evenly.

HEAT large skillet over medium-high heat. Add fish; cook and stir 4 to 5 minutes or until fish flakes easily when tested with fork.

FILL tortillas with fish mixture. Layer with desired toppings. Serve with sour cream sauce.

TIP

For variety, try this recipe with ORTEGA 40% Less Sodium Taco Seasoning and Whole Wheat Tortillas.

Southwest Buffalo Chicken Tacos

MAKES: 4 servings | **PREP:** 5 minutes | **START TO FINISH:** 10 minutes

- **3 tablespoons ORTEGA Taco Sauce, any variety**
- **½ teaspoon cornstarch**
- **7 ounces chunk chicken breast**
- **4 ORTEGA Whole Grain Corn Taco Shells**
- **1 stalk celery, diced**
- **½ cup crumbled blue cheese**

COMBINE taco sauce and cornstarch in small bowl; mix well.

HEAT small skillet over medium heat. Add chicken and taco sauce mixture; stir well. Reduce heat; cook and stir 4 minutes or until mixture has thickened.

DIVIDE filling evenly among taco shells. Top evenly with celery and blue cheese.

Roasted Mexican Corn

MAKES: 6 servings | **PREP:** 5 minutes | **START TO FINISH:** 20 minutes

- **1 bag (16 ounces) frozen corn**
- **2 tablespoons olive oil**
- **½ cup ORTEGA Thick & Chunky Salsa, any variety**
- **1 can (4 ounces) ORTEGA Fire-Roasted Diced Green Chiles**
- **Salt and black pepper, to taste**

TIP

For a great summer side dish, chill the corn before serving. For a hearty salad, add a can of rinsed and drained ORTEGA Black Beans and serve chilled.

PREHEAT oven to 450°F.

PLACE frozen corn in colander; rinse with cold running water to thaw and shake colander to drain well. Press corn between paper towels to remove most of moisture. Place on large rimmed baking sheet; drizzle with oil.

BAKE 10 minutes or until corn begins to turn golden brown. Transfer to medium bowl.

STIR in salsa and chiles; season with salt and pepper. Serve warm.

Spiced Fruit Parfait with Dulce de Leche

MAKES: 8 servings | **PREP:** 15 minutes | **START TO FINISH:** 25 minutes

DULCE DE LECHE

- **1 cup whipping cream**
- **1 cup firmly packed brown sugar**
- **1 teaspoon vanilla**

PARFAIT

- **2 cups diced strawberries**
- **1 cup blueberries**
- **1 cup blackberries**
- **3 tablespoons ORTEGA Taco Seasoning Mix, divided**
- **½ cup whipping cream**
- **8 individual cake dessert shells, diced**

TIP

If you can't find prepared sponge cake dessert shells, use pound cake or any leftover layer cake.

COMBINE 1 cup whipping cream, brown sugar and vanilla in small saucepan; mix well. Bring to a boil over medium-high heat. Reduce heat to medium-low; simmer 5 to 6 minutes or until mixture is reduced by half. Set aside to cool.

COMBINE strawberries, blueberries, blackberries and 2 tablespoons seasoning mix in medium bowl; mix well.

STIR remaining 1 tablespoon seasoning mix into ½ cup whipping cream in chilled bowl. When ready to assemble parfaits, whip mixture with chilled beaters.

PLACE ½ diced cake shell in bottom of each parfait glass; drizzle with about 1½ teaspoons cooled dulce de leche. Top with ¼ cup fruit. Repeat layers and top with dollop of whipped cream. Drizzle with additional dulce de leche, if desired.

Cinnamon Tacos with Fruit Salsa

MAKES: 6 servings | **PREP:** 20 minutes | **START TO FINISH:** 30 minutes

- **1 cup sliced fresh strawberries**
- **1 cup cubed fresh pineapple**
- **1 cup cubed peeled kiwi**
- **½ teaspoon ORTEGA Diced Jalapeños**
- **4 tablespoons plus 1 teaspoon granulated sugar, divided**
- **1 tablespoon ground cinnamon**
- **6 (8-inch) ORTEGA Flour Soft Tortillas**
- **Nonstick cooking spray**

STIR together strawberries, pineapple, kiwi, jalapeños and 4 teaspoons sugar (adjust to taste, if desired) in large bowl; set aside.

COMBINE remaining 3 tablespoons sugar and cinnamon in small bowl; set aside.

COAT tortillas lightly on both sides with nonstick cooking spray. Heat each tortilla in nonstick skillet over medium heat until slightly puffed and golden brown. Remove from heat; immediately dust both sides with cinnamon-sugar mixture. Shake excess cinnamon-sugar back into bowl. Repeat cooking and dusting process until all tortillas are warmed.

FOLD tortillas in half and fill with fruit mixture. Serve immediately.